KU-315-676

R29588

Leeds College
LIBRARY
– 4 DEC 2001
735.291
of Art and Design

Jim Buckley: Fold

21 March — 5 April

Manningham Mills, Bradford

Video projection, computers,

digital software, back projection

Commissioners: Photo 98

A video installation spanning 45 windows and 3 floors of redundant textile mill, Manningham Mills, Bradford. A shuttle of light ran back and forth across the windows, gradually revealing a coloured image, a block of pure colour, or the ghostly film of cloth endlessly folding as it came off the weaving looms.

LEEDS COL OF ART & DESIGN

R29588A0084

"When you're usually really involved with something, you're usually thinking about something else. When something's happening, you fantasise about other things." Andy Warhol.

I am looking for a box amongst a stack of other boxes. In one of these boxes I am trying to find a map which my Grandfather gave to me. It is a map of Yorkshire.¶ I know Yorkshire well as I grew up with it as a view from my home. My home as a three up, three down pebble-dashed terraced house on a modern low rise housing estate in Blackley on the north-eastern side of Manchester. A view looking out of a window and away into a distance that seemed to go on and on forever beyond a dark blue, slate grey stretch of hills called the Pennines.¶ It is the early 1960s, a 'pre-smokeless' age and a mist hangs over the City as the smoke from thousands of tons of burning fossil fuels mingles with the damp steam vapours that rise from the factory chimneys and textile mills. These dilapidated sheds are the final out-posts

of an Industrial Revolution that is just about to breathe its very last breath of such a stale and visibly polluted air.¶ The hills form a fence around the city and separate two neighbouring and traditionally rival counties, Yorkshire the 'White Rose' and Lancashire the 'Red', on one side Yorkshire folk and on the other Lancastrians. It is hard to imagine how these hills could ever have formed a credible boundary between two people who are basically of the same stock. These are the same people who would call a spade a spade, speak of muck as brass and

Felicity Allen: Brief Encounters

1 December — 6 January

St Georges Square, Huddersfield

35mm colour slides

Commissioners: Photo 98

As the light faded each evening in December the eight projectors running the 640 slides for Felicity Allen's Brief Encounters switched on in the windows of offices and shops in the square. The staged sequence of images shows human models shot against brilliant coloured backgrounds and focuses on the detail of everyday gestures of encounters.

refer to the times as hard but say that tram-lines are even harder.¶ The indigenous, slightly shifting Northern population has for centuries mated with a constantly arriving influx of immigrant populations to create a muddle between the two sides that is more than a geological arrangement or a structurally engineered device. It is a way of life.¶ To the people who lived in my house there was no rivalry between us and the people who lived on the other side, as whenever the battles that had been fought had been fought as a war between the two Roses,

our ancestors had all been back home in Ireland fighting a battle *'Fur de wearin',*
o'oh'd green'.¶ *'...fur de wearin' o'oh'd green, o'oh'd wearin o'oh'd green, fur*
de'are hanging men and women now fur de wearin' o'oh'd green.'¶ It is strange to
consider how often a colour will become the evidence of a rivalry, as a 'red' to a
'white' or an 'orange' to a 'green', or as a whole array of flags, pennants, scarves
and rosettes worn or carried as the uniforms and standards of either side.¶ I can
remember a 'Richard of York' who 'Gave Battle In Vain' to become a code for

**Other Worlds: The Iron Way of the
State (Respiratory System - Lungs)**
25-29 November
Cliffords Tower, York
Video projection
Commissioning organisation:
Impressions Gallery (Organic City)

**A 360 degree son et lumiere
projected onto the interior walls
of Clifford's tower combining 3D
animations, film, video and a
soundtrack.**

remembering all of the colours of the rainbow as a red, an orange, a yellow, a green, a blue, an indigo and a violet. This rainbow is a spectrum of coloured light which when focused together re-assembles as white. And white as a light is a deceptive notion of purity, cleanliness and a supposed calm and peaceable

Paul Bradley:

Tomorrow, forever and never

1 January — 31 December

Dean Clough, Halifax

12 7x6cm projection transparencies

Commissioners: Photo 98

Overlaying the architectural facade of Dean Clough an historical and now contemporary landmark, with the image of a burning candle, which gradually appeared to burn down as the year progressed until all that was left was a ghostly flickering image on the final day of the year.

resolution.¶ Yorkshire was never white to me, it was always green. A 'greener-grass' and just across the way from where we lived, a view out, over and across on to the other side, twenty minutes by train, forty minutes by coach or up to an hour on the school minibus.¶ We went there on special trips to see Beauty Spots and to

Gina Czarnecki: Versifier
Ferens Art Gallery, Hull
3 — 12 October
Video projection, mirror
Commissioner: Hull Time Based Arts
(Lucid)

**In a closed ante-chamber entered
through a mirrored door, a
triangular space of 30 naked
human forms gradually start to
come to life, moving and mutating.**

study those landmarks which had been marked as having a particular social,
industrial or religious importance. We wrote essays on the Brontes, (spell-check:
Brunettes) describing the effects of the 'wildness' and 'ruggedness' of the
landscape around their home in Haworth and how the emotional struggle between
Heathcliffe and Catherine was reflected by Emily in her vivid description of the
Moors.¶ For those pupils less romantically inclined there was the alternative essay
title to describe in no more than 250 words the Coming of Steam and its importance

for the lives of ordinary people living in the area.¶ As I find the box I can see where I have previously scrawled in a blue biro 'Grandad's Maps'. The box is tatty looking, the lustre has tarnished but the letters are still boldly embossed to proudly proclaim that Terry's are All Gold.¶ Terry's of York. Terry's as a plain chocolate was a name to conjure with at a time when plain automatically meant posh. If Terry's would have battled with Cadbury's, they might have procured the brand name of Roses for themselves and re-united the Kingdom under a great confectionery banner, Terry's — an All Golden Rose. ¶ We bought the chocolates for

Flocked.

An evening projection
by Lulu Quinn

Lulu Quinn: Flocked

House of Fraser shop window,
Sheffield

14 March — 26 April

Video projection

Commissioners: Lovebytes

(Hypertribes)

**An interactive video installation.
A sheep gazes at passers-by from
the window of a department
store, mirroring their movement.
Looks are exchanged, the sheep
observes without regard.
The moment passes; audience
and sheep retreat to other spaces.**

my mother. She loved the gesture but hated plain chocolates. So we melted them

Heather Ackroyd and Dan Harvey:
Photosynthesis: Testament
The Old Icehouse, Hull
28 August — 13 September
Grass
Commissioner: Hull Time Based Arts
(Lucid)

Young grass shoots produce a highly sensitive surface in which an image can be printed in chlorophyll. The equivalent tonal range developed within black and white photographic paper is created within the grass photograph in shades of yellow and green. Set within the Old Icehouse, a 20ft portrait of an elderly woman was the focus of the living grass installation.

down, boiled them all up with extra sugar, half a packet of butter and a tin of sweetened condensed milk to produce a delicious home-made fudge. The mess

GHOST
IN
THE
NETWORK

The National Centre for Popular Music, situated in the former site of Kennings' Garage in Sheffield is anticipating an annual 400,000 visitors in 1999 alone. Designed like a sprawling internet site, its 15 million pounds' worth of guts is hooked up by a centrally driven computer system. In the atrium, metres of conspicuous orange piping function as a skeleton frame to support the building's glass exterior. The themed rooms that spin off like hotlinks from its centre serve up high tech ambisonic surround sound, interactive touch videos and high speed 3D visuals. The NCPM would have undoubtedly done proud the region's now disbanded public slogan 'Sheffield Shines'. Yet the only clue that points to Sheffield's manufacturing history is the four towering cowes positioned on top of the structure. Aptly made from steel, the poles function as environmentally-friendly air conditioning, whilst unsentimentally nodding to Sheffield's past as the world's forerunner of steel. But whereas 'Sheffield Shines' left most grimacing as it issued a nostalgic and hollow echo to the region's former glory, the NCPM operates as a model of new technology, in which audiences can experience both past and present spliced seamlessly together. It stands as a gleaming user-friendly monument to the changing lifestyles, shifting populations and cultural transformations that have impacted on the region since the turn of the Industrial Revolution and the laying of rail tracks in the 19th century.

The Centre symbolises a significant move away from the twinning of old and new that has characterised much of the way that the Yorkshire and Humberside regions have been described since de-industrialisation in the 1960s. Derelict sites, redundancies and pit, mill and factory closures have not only helped to sever the old manufacturing industries and social customs from the shiny digitised new, but have also left gaping holes that have been plugged up with sensationalist stories that reek of the loss of the past. Former mining village Grimethorpe grabbed recent headlines with *'Miner's children in the pits of heroin.'* The only prevailing industry in the devastated community was drugs trafficking. Alongside the media's heavy-handed mythic representation of the past, come new developments aided

went everywhere, traces of chocolate in our hair, on our clothes, on the towels and worst of all a particularly stubborn stain on one of the new stretch sofa cushion

and abetted by information technology. The networks of fibre optic cables that lurk invisibly underground in shallow trenches and the generic banality of the shopping mall with its CCTV methods of surveillance and controlling consumers enforces the view that those older manufacturing spaces that sustained and gave meaning to local communities have collapsed and been replaced almost entirely by private interests. Key to this is the misleading notion that history is a linear, progressive series of events marked by technological revolutions. The increasing pile of cultural and real debris can only be cleaned up by raw banks of virtual information supplied by a new influx of high tech tools.

Another outcome of the twinning of old and new is the transformation of tourists into amateur historians who consume by excavating the past and play witness to the derelict monuments of the industrial past. Witness Hebden Bridge, a town in Yorkshire that boomed at the start of the Industrial Revolution, saw its textile factories either bankrupt, closed or merged throughout the 1960s and 70s. History is now its principal raw economic material; a promo web site testifies to the polishing and packaging of its heritage; over the old chemist's shop, a new information centre has been built to service tourism; the visitor can plan a trail from the hillsides on which E P Thompson, author of The Making of the English Working Class, first researched the traumatic erasure of handloom weaving on a 200 year-old derelict mill that ran on waterpower until the trains brought coal in and businesses were subsequently moved nearer to the railhead. Crafts and memorabilia, from hand-

loomed textiles to factory produced corduroys, can be bought at the Mill Shop on Albert Street. Hebden Bridge is marketed as a living history, utilising information media to enable its countless, fragmented stories — from the 18th century weavers to those labourers in the sewing shops in the 1930s — to be continually recounted.

Whilst digital technologies can revive lost histories, it is this manufactured twinning of old and new that masks the real legacies left by the industries that have inherently imprinted the Yorkshire and Humberside regions. As opposed to the sudden transformation of old to new, the relationship should be seen as more of an evolutionary change, one which is fuelled by new technologies. The virtual space of the Internet, with its nodes and hotlinks allowing travel and connection to disparate communities sees its direct descendent in the swell of immigrants moving towards the booming manufacturing industries. The boundaries of Yorkshire were initially fixed by the identity of a specific industry, but as the railways and other methods of shifting product were constructed, so communities would disperse in wider, looser networks. George Hudson's railway in York in 1839, for example, gave employment to 5,500 people directly and several thousand more in the manufacturing industries that grew around them. The communities then brought in with the promise of work needed churches, banks, offices, schools and colleges. More than 150 years later, the fibre-optic cables that were laid parallel the importing and exporting of goods in the form of goods or data. Links between the weaving of the textile trades and the computer's ability to knit together binary coding also assembles a legacy that points to the circularity of history. It subsequently rings true that regions that saw the demise of the manufacturing industries should equally evolve into prime new technological sites of digital activity.

covers. The gesture had got out of hand but my mother didn't mind, she saw it as a test for her new biological washing powder.¶ *'But what is biological, Mum?'*¶

But it is not simply technology reinventing the wheel. Those industrial landscapes were ideal for evolutionary processes to work themselves out. What is little known about these regions that have been characterised as *'technologically creative'* is that it was the structural frameworks of the communities and not a heavy investment into new technologies that steered the industries to boom. In Yorkshire, the woollen trade surpassed competitors internationally because of its ability to appropriate and adapt technologies for the clothiers own interests. In the 18th century, clothiers, for example, adopted the

spinning jenny for use in their own homes and gained access to more expensive technologies through the use of public mills. The merchants were linked to a flexible production network of thousands of clothiers working from their own homes. The Taylors were a Leeds-based family of clothiers who manufactured, dyed and dealt in cloth in the nineteenth century. Leaders in the economic activities of the community, their plans to open a bank and build local public cloth mills that would be rented out to small firms enabled them to be seen not as outsiders but apart of a community. In this way, whole communities were seen as self-organising systems, that rejected centrally-controlled production and marketing systems that characterised their main competitors and set them apart as world leaders. It is this framework of community structure that has left its traces.

These disguised legacies — the ghosts in the network, help illuminate the cracks between the twinning of new and old technologies. Society is techno-schizophrenic: we believe in the inevitability of progress, whilst controlling it to fit into pre-existing social patterns. When Prime Minister Thatcher was reported in the Economist to be making *'the most major decision since the Industrial Revolution'* to lay cable wires in 1982, it is perhaps telling that five years later cable penetration comprised a mere 1.25% of the nation. In fact, those first networks laid in Yorkshire and Humberside only occurred at the turn of this decade. Nor have fibre optics transformed communities into a glut of homogeneous slack-jawed consumers as was predicted in some quarters. The widely held view that communities are said to draw upon socialisation within a global media, as electronic media undermines a sense of geographic and cultural place, is sharply counteracted by the fact that the media industries in Yorkshire are steadfastly serving the region's own interests. As part of Kirklees' cultural initiatives programme, a media centre was opened in the mid nineties to serve community interests and was

networked by Cabletel. South Yorkshire was given the status of being one of the most deprived areas in the European Union in 1988 alongside a report from Demos that suggested it as a potential 'cultural industry capital'. Subsequently the council launched the region's Cultural Industries Quarter, now home to the NCPM.

Competitive advantage in the Yorkshire and Humberside region was never founded exclusively on the influx of new tools into industry, rather on combining the region's surviving community structures with copying and borrowing new products. It is this legacy that so rarely surfaces in debates around the twinning of old and new that now steers the regions not to a new beginning, but one whose position will be as key to the information industries as manufacturing was to its past.

Caroline Smith

She looked bemused by the question and then turned to read the side of the packet.¶ 'It *has to do with enzymes. They attack dirt in the wash and eat it.'*¶

'*But what about chocolate Mum, will they eat that?*'¶ As it turned out they did, and as it also turned out they continued to feast their appetites on my flesh. For years I suffered from eczema which was later diagnosed as an allergic reaction to the enzymes in biological washing powders.¶ I stayed in for much of the time that I was ill and watched so much television that my dreams became extensions of T.V., serial dramas including the commercial breaks. ¶ The austerity of post-war Britain gave way in the 1960s and 1970s to the resurgence of a concept known as a

Lifestyle. And our Lifestyle was formed around a range of popular images.¶ This is the time when Lichtenstein took Pop imagery from comic magazines and Warhol collected Brillo boxes and Campbell's soup cans from supermarkets. This is also a time when my mum re-invented us children as space cadets. She chopped off most of our hair, blow-dried and lacquered the rest until our hair-dos had become convincing versions of space helmets. And my Dad added to the routine by making us fantastic plastic outfits to wear from the Crimplene, Terylene and Duralene off-

**Matthew Maxwell: Boggarts
(Immune System)**

Unspecified sites all over York

June

Hologram and glass

Commissioning organisation:

Impressions Gallery (Organic City)

**5000 glass semi-spheres
embedded with a holographic
image of a teddy bear holding a
grenade were distributed
throughout York over a period of
5 days intended to be freely
collected and removed by
whoever found them.**

cuts from the factory where he worked.¶ We were Evaprest and Stayprest into a
look that was not so much based on the genuine appearance of space-men, who
were by now actually landing on the Moon, what we were modelled on was a former
B-Movie generation of original spacemen, who were themselves only the

descendants of an earlier generation of Fritz Lang characters from the film

Metropolis.¶ My Mother and Father must have copied their designs from so many

other versions of copy after copy. But at this time that was very much the vogue as

Mary Quant would copy her New Look from the images of Louise Brooks in the Pabst

Abdul Qualam Aziz: Defending the Realm (Muscular System - Muscles)

Station Rd, City Walls, York

19 September - 31 December

Silk-screen, fabric, wood

Commissioning organisation:

Impressions Gallery (Organic City)

Two double-sided framed photographically silk-screened images of guardsmen taken from four different time-spans (Roman, Angle, Norman, Medieval), represent the armoury, muscular structure and defence mechanisms.

films Diary of a Lost Girl and Pandora's Box and the Beatles were only a slightly less raffish version of some Edwardian ponce.¶ The mass-produced and subsequently reproduced image of ourselves as players in a Modern Lifestyle was set against a backdrop of a Futuristic adventure that seemed to suggest a way of referring ourselves forward but in fact we were only parodying a cinematic past. We were a Bri-nylon version of the Family Von Trapp.¶ I find myself going up and down and in between the aisles of a supermarket lost amid the sea of slogans and

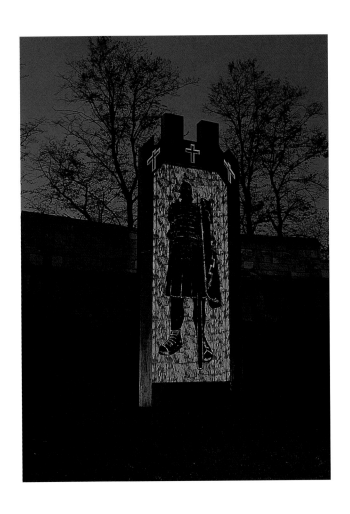

star bursting motifs. I am a hesitant shopper, I ponder over every purchase. There are so many piles and so many people picking at those piles, and where they have chosen to take from a space appears which other people fill, rapidly fill-up with more of what looks like some more of the same perfectly formed satsumas or fun-sized bananas, peaches or pears.¶ I have to check out the specials, sell-by dates and cooking times. Decide on whether or not I should oven, grill or micro-wave, freeze, boil in the bag, heat in the carton, remove the lid or pierce the film. Is it

Bluntcut: Preset Softwar Version

1.0: Psychostasia

(Urinary System - Bowels)

27 November

CD Rom

Web site

Stone carving

Commissioning organisation:

Impressions Gallery (Organic City)

**A CD Rom, interactive game and
a web site exploring issues
around the erotic attraction of
death, and a web site
accompanied by a stone bearing
the legend: www.bluntcut.com
installed beside ancient tomb
stones near the Multangular
Tower, York.**

on or off the bone? Does it contain nuts? Is it easy to carve, pre-basted for extra

succulence, lo-salt, bio-lite, semi-skimmed, virtually fat free, just a gentle soak,

rinsed well, washed and ready to serve? Will it act as an ideal accompaniment to a chicken, fish or a suitable vegetarian dish?¶ On this particular journey I am

looking for a stain-remover. The stain is there as the result of an accident.

Although I would assume that most stains are there, wherever they are, as the

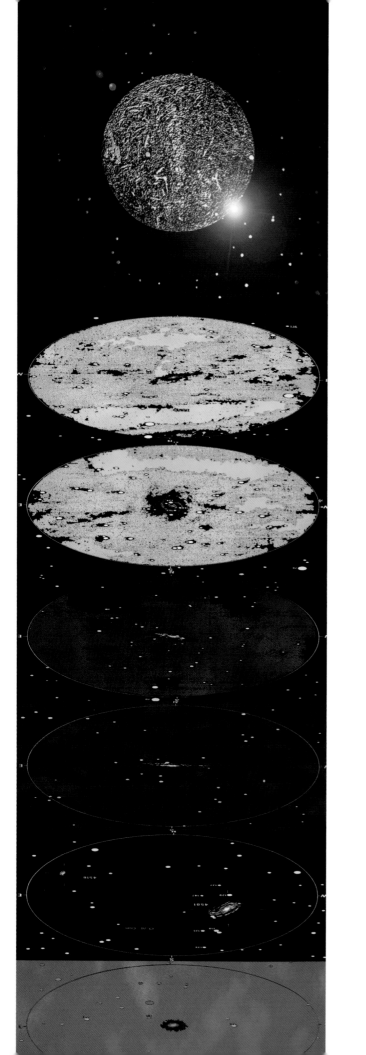
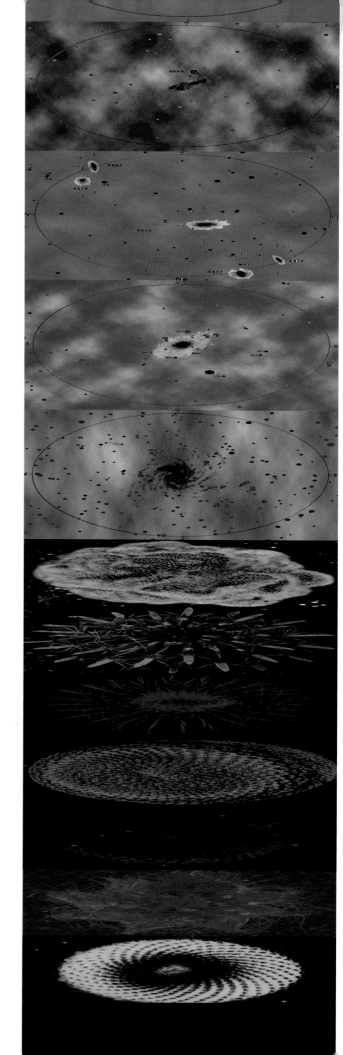

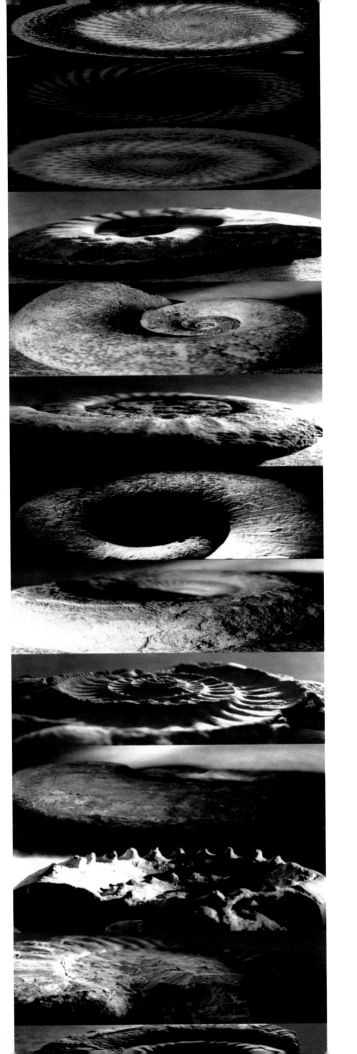
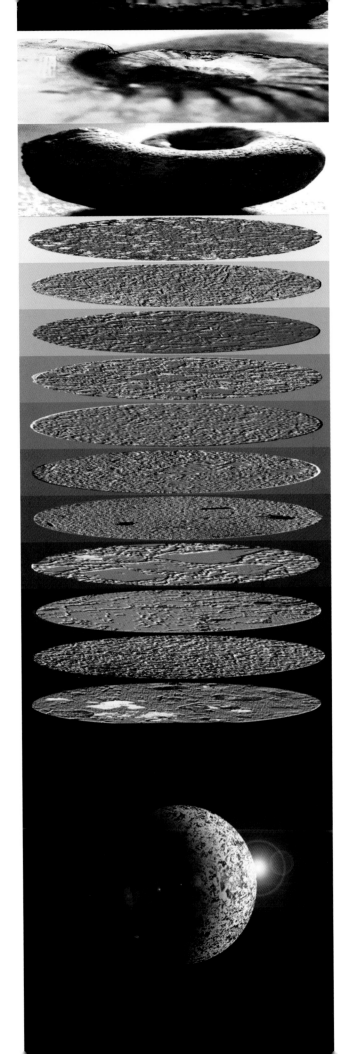

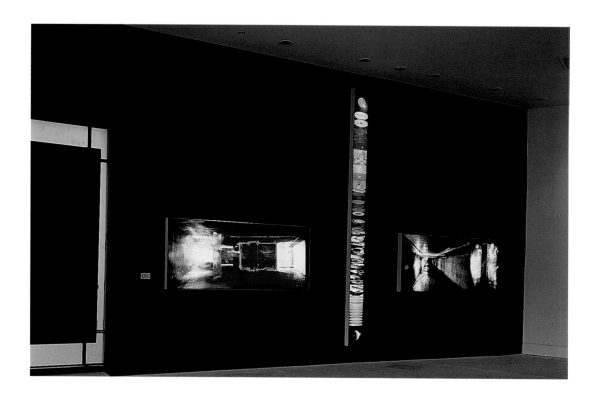

Helen Sear: Labyrinth, Strata
The Earth Centre, Conisbrough
Permanent
Lightboxes
Co-commission The Earth Centre
and Photo 98

Three light boxes located in the main entrance to the Planet Earth Pavilion in the new environmental attraction, The Earth Centre. Strata is a thin continuous image showing 39 sections of an imagined cross section of the earth and beyond representing organic fragments of heat, fire, water, ice and wind. Labyrinth is a pair of large scale lightboxes 'imaging' the heating system below the ground, based on an ancient Roman principle 'to light fire from below'. The work visually 'lights the fire' conjuring up the story of the Minatour, using light and figures to articulate the architectural space and referring to temperature with colour. Labyrinth is 'performative' photographic tableaux.

result of an accident. And this particular stain is amongst the most stubborn to

Stefan Gec: Twins: Twins
Doncaster Station
Permanent
Photographs
Commissioning organisation:
Impressions Gallery (On-Line)

A permanently sited lightbox at Doncaster station, based on the town's relationship with its twin towns of Gliwice, Poland and Wilmington, North Carolina, USA.

shift. It is a trace of myself, of my human self, like blood, shit, sweat, grease etc. ¶

**Mark Wallinger: The Hour When
Railway Lines Meet at Infinity**
Railway Carriage on Platform 7,
Sheffield Station
24 October — 20 November
Video projection
Commissioner: Site Gallery, Sheffield
(Shunted)

**A video projection filmed in the
gloom and illumination of a Circle
Line underground train and
shown in the corresponding space
of a train carriage on Platform 7
of the Station.**

TCR 01:31:16:08

But in the supermarket I am reminded that this stain is most often referred to as dirt or, in washing powder terminology, as soil.¶ I have a heavy soil on a delicate fabric.¶ After a time I expect that this trace (a trace of myself), would accumulate an evidence of the continuous passage of my self, not only moving across, but forever and ever sinking deeper and deeper into and underneath this surface. And I wonder about those days, and then the days after those days when all of the liquid that might seep from my body would be taken back and absorbed into the

Samantha Clark:

Culture (Reproduction)

Parliament Street, York

10 October – 31 December

Double-sided lightbox

Commissioning organisation:

Impressions Gallery (Organic City)

A double-sided light box illustrating the slow growth of the city. The growth of the settlement of York is matched by the digital reproduction of human cells, pictured frame by frame in a weekly cycle.

ground where it could ferment to become a liquorous libation to the sodden Earth. And suddenly a jingle plays over in my mind.¶ If the stain says hot but the label says not...¶ But what then, what follows on from that, a 'something, something', a 'something something' that would 'make the difference'. What is it, the brand

**Samantha Clark: Culture
(Digestive System)**
Four Public Toilets in York City Centre
1 - 31 December
Light boxes
Commissioning organisation:
Impressions Gallery (Organic City)

**Mimicking the journey food takes
as it passes through our bodies,
a series of diagrams making
reference to public transport
maps were paired with medical
images of the digestive organs
displayed in light boxes at the
entrance to selected public toilets
in York.**

name that I am looking for? It is well known, either Bold, Persil or Aerial. ¶ If the stain says hot but the label says not, Bold makes the difference. ¶ If the stain says hot but the label says not, then Persil will make the difference.¶ That sounds better but just one more try.¶ If the stain says hot but the label says not, then

**Richard Hylton: Heroes and Foes
(Endocrine System - Hormones)**
On sale at various retail outlets in
York
4th October - 31 December
removable tattoos
Commissioning organisation:
Impressions Gallery (Organic City)

**A series of removable tattoos
representing plausible and
implausible heroes and foes
nominated by members of the
public, included : Dickie Bird,
Arthur Scargill, Alan Rickman,
McDonalds, Nelson Mandela,
Adolf Hitler, Mahatama Ghandi
and Mao Tse Tung.**

Aerial makes the difference. ¶ It sounds just the same as Persil. I can't choose.¶

Somewhere I am trying to recall a spring meadow trying to hear if the slogan will

match up to an image in my mind. As I do I find my hands have inadvertently

Mongrel: National Heritage

Web site, newspaper and poster

Mongrel presentation: Saturday

10th October, Hull Screen

Commissioner: Hull Time Based Arts

(Lucid)

National Heritage is a project put
together by Harwood and
Matthew Fuller taking on the use
of new communications
technology for the dissemination
and organisation of various
forms of eugenics, nationalism
and racism. Mongrel hacks onto
a popular search engine. When
any searches are made on that
engine for racist material the
user gets dumped into a parallel
network of web-sites set up by
Mongrel.

wandered away from me like two naughty children, and lifted up a product called

Stain Devil. As my thoughts are now some way behind my actions, I can no longer

think straight.¶ Two white sheets bounce up and down on the washing line with a

Andrew Stones:
Provincially / Provisionally
Sheffield Town Hall Extension
14 March — 26 April
Neon
Commissioners: Lovebytes
(Hypertribes)

Fifteen flashing signs in yellow
neon for the exterior of Sheffield
Town Hall Extension. The phrases
reflect something of the nature
of civic language.

couple of fleecy bath towels that are too heavy to bounce so they just flap about.
And I think that I can see an aura, an amazing after-glow and can smell a

springtime freshness. This clean, clear, intoxicating scent wafts through my mind

causing me to take a sudden sharp intake of my own breath. There is some kind of

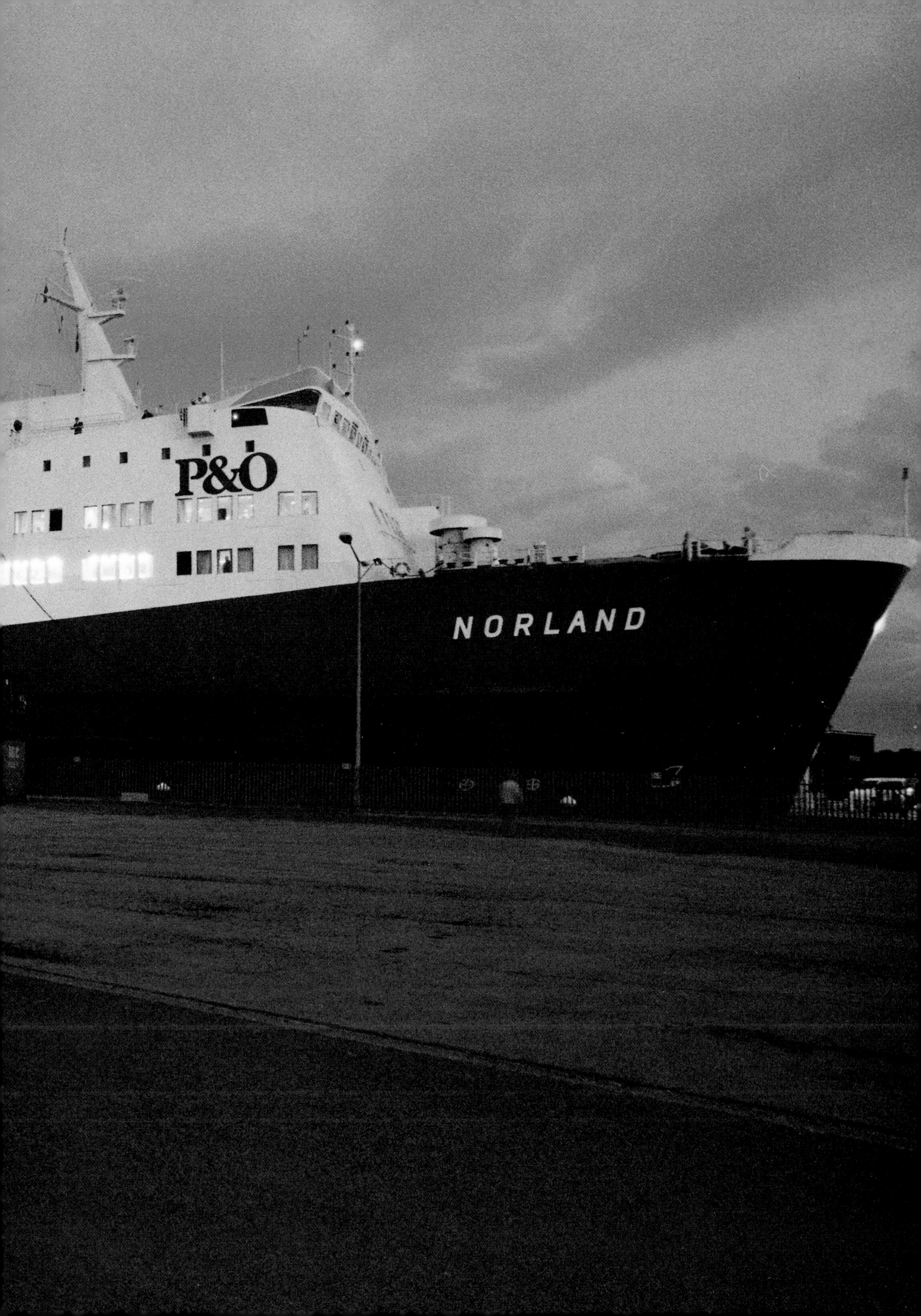
P&O
NORLAND

PREVIOUS SPREAD / LEFT

**Andy Hazell with Carolyn
Mendelsohn: Lumina**
King George's Dock
10 - 11 October
Video projection
Commissioner: Hull Time Based Arts
(Lucid)

**Twin video projections onto the
side of the departing P & O Ferry
leaving Hull docks for Rotterdam
and Zeebrugge, drawn from
archive material of the thousands
of immigrants arriving in Hull on
the Wilson Line at the turn of the
century. The event was staged at
dusk over two nights
accompanied by live music,
vodka, borscht and bagels.**

nature re-freshed here as a reminder of a season that has never existed except as an arrangement on a shelf.¶ The box is untied, the string just slipped away and there right on the top of the pile is Yorkshire:¶ Yorkshire and the Ridings.¶ I

Simon Poulter: Hyperphilately

Main Post Office, Fitzalan Square,
Sheffield
www.hypertribes.org.uk/hyperphilately
14 March — 26 April
Vinyl banner and website
Commissioners: Lovebytes (Hypertribes)

Internet users and visitors to
Sheffield's City Centre were invited
to collect 34 original stamps from
the website, one each day. The work
also featured the largest digital
stamp ever made which hung from
Sheffield's main Post Office.

wonder what the Ridings are, have they all gone, vanished as part of the same

reorganisation that made London and Manchester into Greater places and Liverpool

into a Side?¶ The map looks old and smells smelly. As I unfold each rectangular

Chumpon Apisuk: En Route

21 September - 10 october

Fly posters and residency

Commissioner: Hull Time Based Arts

(Lucid)

A short residency resulting in a series of fly posters. Local people were invited to pose in front of a typical Hull scene pictured with their suitcase en route, replicating the stereotypical images used by local authorities to promote the culture of their cities.

section little bits fall away, Skipton and Ilkley are torn off completely, stuck on to the message side of a postcard which was stuck on to the map.¶ *'Dear Mam and Dad, Have arrived safely, journey not too bad. Weather's fine. Kids enjoying everything. The caravan site is right next door to a big Butlin's so Richard and I got out for a drink last night with Don and Olive. As you can see there is a huge billiard room here so Richard is very happy. With lots of love. Barbara. p.s. We look forward to seeing you both on Friday'.*¶ 'Barbara' my mother's name. I turn over the card to

see where We are.¶ BUTLIN'S FILEY — A Billiard Room. Photo: E. Nagele, John Hinde

Studios.¶   Judging by the clothes and hairstyles it must be... Yes! it is 1966. A

holiday in Butlin's as the view from the picture side of a postcard.¶   A big green

billiard table takes up the entire foreground and about 50% of the whole size of the image. Two strong, straight/straightish lines form an inwardly pointing diagonal track which takes my eyes up either side of the table toward the first horizontal plane which forms the top end of the table. This line is about two thirds of the way up the height of a landscape composition. And along the line the backside of a man in a light blue sweater shifts the focus of my attention from the foreground toward the back of the room as he bends over ready to play.¶ There are fourteen red balls, a pink, a green, a blue, a yellow, a brown, a black and a white ball spread amazingly evenly across a green baize cover. A girl in a vivid pink and what looks like an angora sweater competes with the backside of the man in the light blue sweater for the visual pull. She has the advantage of showing us her face as she places her cue just behind the white ball. She is playing with a couple, a girl and a boy who are holding on to their own cues as they try to fix their 'as if' attentive gaze, as firmly as they might on to her tip, as she is about to pop her first shot.¶ As this is clearly a game of doubles, two cues, four cues but never ever

three, there is obviously a missing cue, a missing partner. Someone is not visible

within the parameters of this frame. Perhaps he or she has nipped away, gone off

**Ann Whitehurst with
Patrick Courtney and
Harry Palmer: Dependent**
Throughout October
On line research project and live
event

Ann Whitehurst carried out
research (`Loosenews`) which then
evolved in to the web site
`Dependent` playing on language
in relation to disability.

to the toilet or to the bar to get a round of drinks in or whatever. But why wouldn't
they have held on for just a little while longer to see her take this shot. It is an

**Impossible Theatre
(Chris Squire and Charlotte
Diefenthal): Destined**
Central Concourse
24 October — 20 November
Information display boards
Commissioner: Site Gallery, Sheffield
(Shunted)

**A pair of electromagnetic flip dot
matrix information boards display
a succession of constantly
shifting messages. These
messages originate from a series
of workshops with people from
Sheffield: a group retraining after
acquiring disability through
accident or illness; Somali people
who have recently moved to the
city; an Age Concern group.
Thoughts and experiences have
also been elicited from people in
and around the station —
commuters, trainspotters, visitors
and local passengers.**

important move as she has either potted the first red, as one of the reds is missing,

and is now chasing a colour in which case she is snookered, or this is her first shot

against the opponents who must have failed to follow on from potting their first

red.¶ Or else I could imagine that I am the missing partner, as it is me holding on

Lisa Erdman: Ethnimage
Princes Quay Shopping Centre, Hull
11th October
Performance
Commissioner: Hull Time Based Arts
(Lucid)

The artist makes a sales pitch in a
shopping centre parodying
American-style shopping channel
T.V., alerting us to assumptions
made concerning racial identity
and physical traits.

to the card. I am in the same position as the photographer, where he or she must

have stood in order to place the camera. Perhaps this is why I find the postcard so

CONDITIONS OF USE - PARTICIPATION IN OLD AND NEW MEDIA

appealing, it is as if I am still there where I have (I am now assuming), already

been.¶   The map is in ruins. A mouldy growth has spread as a fungal forest

There is an identifiable historical moment when any new technology develops a sense of self-awareness. This is not artificial intelligence, not an awareness on the part of the technology itself, but a moment when the adoption of that technology reaches a saturation point that permits a perspective on its own conditions and uses. This moment often coincides with the broadening of access to this technology, with the shift from lab to commodity, from research user to home user. The moment when technologies find a place in everyday life, even if only in the everyday life of a privileged few early adopters, is when they begin to attain a cultural importance that can be interrogated of itself, without reference to their primary function.

This is a kind of perversion of technology, or at least it appears to be so from the viewpoint of the inventors and pioneers that first adopted it. It is a form of emancipation from original purpose, a 'coming out' into the embrace of a larger audience with political, social, and economic assumptions about what the future uses of the technology will bring.

The primary media technologies of the twentieth century - Photography, Film, Radio, Television, Video - have grown up in this way, moving from exotic spectacle to diverse, ubiquitous presence, from the awe-inspiring to the mundane. As technologies are commodified and marketed, their increasingly streamlined mainstream products leave behind them a wake of discrete practices - an aftershock of adaptive techniques that consciously or unconsciously turn prescribed instructions into a new vocabulary of habits and rituals.

As soon as the photograph moved from being a studio-bound appointment into a stolen snapshot, it was freed to develop an infinite new variety of uses, from historical record to forensic evidence to memento mori. The history of photography could never be traced in straight lines from the hybrid scientific/cultural activities of its pioneers. There could never be an accurate audit of its impact, as every discarded photo-booth snapshot is a fork in the path of it development as a cultural object in a fragmented social arena.

'At the threshold points near the birth of new technology, all types of distortions and misunderstandings are bound to appear – misunderstandings not only of how the machines actually work but also of more subtle matters - what realm of experience the new technologies belong to, what values they perpetuate, where their more indirect efforts will take place.'(1)

Like the photograph, whose history of 'distortions and misunderstandings' stretches from Man Ray to Cindy Sherman, the development of computer interfaces has begun to fragment through the speed of its technical development and mass utilisation. Its presumed invisibility as a tool has begun to be challenged, in the way that the photograph shifted from being a 'pencil of nature' to a contingent and fugitive document of the 'real'.

The opaque languages of early computing, the punch cards and command line interfaces that were impenetrable to anybody but their inventors, gradually gave way to a succession of interfaces that attempted to correspond more accurately to the experiences of a mass audience. From Ivan Sutherland's Sketch pad to Doug Engelbart's ground-breaking development of Graphical User Interfaces (GUIs), the computer interface has sought to camouflage its infinitely intricate processes with a visual language of icons, windows and menus. And like photography, this language aspires to become a 'second nature', a metaphor for lived experience that develops its own currency and uses. In the case of most contemporary operating systems, the metaphors of desktop, folders and wastebasket operate as signposts to assist the virtual navigation of stored data. But like photography, the assumed neutrality of these

throughout the whole of the East Riding and turned Hull into nothing more than a grey suggestion. Blackburn has over-printed in reverse like a satanic code onto a

representations disguise the conditions of their creation and the tangled histories of trial and error that belie the uniformity of their surfaces. Computers are not built as perfect vessels, but are palimpsests, like cities. Hardware and software systems cannibalise successful elements, perpetuating historical conditions as if they were genetic traits. As the Y2K bug demonstrates, the complexity of digital systems causes mutation as well as innovation, burying errors within a history of use that renders them virtually invisible.

But there is an important distinction between the interface and previous forms of media technology. The photographic message (according to Barthes) is contingent on its means of production, dissemination and consumption, but repeated exposures offer more or less the same set of contingencies, affected only by historical processes. The photograph's possible meaning is dependent on exterior associations - the context of display (newspaper, magazine, poster) or annotation (caption), but these rarely affect the surface of the photograph itself.

With the interface, the disruption of its surface is the only way that meaning can be produced. Shifting icons, arranging files and personalising the data space is not only allowed, but essential to using the interface. To quote Andreas Broeckmann, *Participation becomes not only an option, but a condition*(2). But this participation has to operate within the boundaries defined by the interface, by the protocols of data transmission that allow a series of ones and zeros to be represented as an image file, a text document or a web page. Any transgression of these protocols result in error messages that only serve to make the user aware of the limits of knowledge. The interface shifts intermittently between vehicle and obstacle, a tentative series of steps mapped out by the user with every point and click.

In this way the act of participation is never as final as it is with a photographic click of a camera shutter, but actually 'conditions' the object into a format that is more amenable to the user. The click of the mouse does not have the same gravity as Barthes' formula for the photograph as an interface between Life/Death, but is a series of subtle

shifts - not necessarily a progression, but still a form of movement. With the extent of this personalisation - from setting your own desktop to hacking and 'open source' software development - the interface develops through a process of 'auto-ergonomics', a process that embodies post-structuralist assumptions about author-reader interaction in a way that static media could only begin to describe.

I would now like to look at three examples of the interface as cultural object, three projects that examine the status of the interface as a fluid map, as a conditional yet mobile network of associative meanings. All of these projects attempt to make visible the production of meaning through the many participative moments of the user - the hundreds of point-and-clicks that define the relationship between interface and user. In this process, some parallels can be noted between the critical enquiry of the singular click of the photograph and the many clicks of the contemporary interactive experience.

IOD - THE WEB STALKER

'The Web Stalker establishes that there are other potential cultures of use for the web. The aesthetic conventions of current Browsers are based on the discipline of Human Computer Interface Design [...] Here, the normal user is only ever the normalised user. Time to mutate.'(3)

Some of the most recent net.art(4) attempts to foreground the means of production in a medium that has, in a very short time, become more opaque under increasingly commercial influences. What was once a low-tech community medium using basic textual communication has become a son et lumiere spectacle

dampened patch of tea-stained paper formerly known as Doncaster. Rotherham is attached to Scunthorpe and Buxton is stuck under the enormous weight of a

that is being hyped as the future of entertainment, commerce and consumption. The Web Stalker opens up the elemental nodes and network possibilities of the web that have become hidden underneath the glossy surfaces of corporate web design.

Contemporary browsers such as Navigator and Explorer reassure the novice user with references to older cultural forms, referring to web 'pages' that can be navigated 'back and forwards' or 'bookmarked'. The Web Stalker takes a singular node on the network (a URL provided by the user) and presents the connections extending from this as an ever-growing diagram of points and lines. By offering hard data, visualised as a map rather than contained in metaphor, the Web Stalker demonstrates the untidy connections, false links and anarchic possibilities of a medium that ultimately thrives on connection rather than closure. The Web Stalker demonstrates the infinite potential for meaning within networks without attempting to second guess the user's own choices. The much-hyped interactivity of digital technologies is not 'guided' by animated icon helpers, but presented as a stark skeleton - a map without an index.

MONGREL - NATURAL SELECTION

'The idea is to pull the rug from underneath racist material on the net, and also to start eroding the perceived neutrality of information science type systems. If people can start to imagine that a good proportion of the net is faked then we might start getting somewhere.'(5)

If the Web Stalker reveals the Internet as an arbitrary, anarchic map of connections, Natural Selection uses the (im)possibilities of accessing these connections as a metaphor for the frustrations caused by 'institutionalised' racism in the UK. Natural Selection also perverts the conventions of the Web browser, but in a subtler way, not stripping the interactive experience of metaphor, but twisting the user's expectations of the metaphor. Resembling the common search engine 'Yahoo', Natural selection deals with user's search requests in two ways. Most searches are directed straight to a 'normal' engine that processes the results and returns lists of options. But if the search contains one of a list of racially suspect words (eg. nigger, nazi, paki), then Natural Selection refers the search to its own database of sites, such as Mervin Jarman's BAA, a site that in turn perverts a corporate site to give the user a feeling for the vagaries of the British immigration system.

In BAA, users enter data to gauge whether they are allowed to gain access to the UK (BAA standing for British Airport Authority, the body in charge of UK airport security). The questions start to give a clue of the interface's perversion, asking if the visitor is travelling on business, pleasure, or to smuggle drugs. As the user works through the long list of questions, the interrogation breaks down, lapsing into patois and becoming more and more bizarre. Depending on the user's 'status', the site then sends you to reports documenting real-life experiences of violence and mistreatment by BAA staff and police to Afro-Caribbean travellers.

Mongrel's abuse of 'official' interfaces peels back the veneer of neutrality that interfaces are assumed to have in the way that artists like Maud Sulter interrogated the photograph in the 1980's. By their very nature, interfaces filter information and make assumptions about the needs of the user, but the logic that informs these decisions can carry with them 'cultural' prejudices that can exclude options for the user in the same way the immigration processes exclude visitors. The increasingly commercial pressure on the Internet means that most users appreciation of the Web's diversity is constricted by

'caramelised' strip of sellotape. 'Hali' and 'fax' are two divided states caught on a fold and only joined by the intervening attachment of a thin linen thread that acts

the databases and classification of 'portal' sites like Yahoo or Excite. Mongrel opens up these processes of classification, using their own tactical interventions to disrupt the smooth surfaces of corporate webspace.

SAWAD BROOKS - LAPSES AND ERASURES

If the interface is, as Steven Johnson has suggested, the cultural form of the very late 20th Century, then it is navigation, the participation between author and audience, that legitimises the interface as a cultural experience. The audience has gradually got closer and closer to the screen throughout the century, from the darkened audience sitting twenty feet away from the cinema screen, to the six feet between sofa and television in the average domestic space. With interactive experiences, the audience is typically less than a foot away from the screen, and with immersive VR experiences this distance is almost completely abolished. Marketing departments in multi-media corporations use the terms 'lean-forward' and 'lean-back' to describe the difference between passive viewing and interactive experience. One of the major obstacles in the development of convergent media such as Web-TV is the audiences' unwillingness to shift between these modes of experience. In fact, it is beginning to seem that mass consumer products using interactive technologies may not only appear through the predicted route of broadband TV/PC hybrids, but also through the personalised, intimate and already interactive technologies used in mobile communications. These products have a very different relationship to the body, slung in holsters like guns or tools, and increasingly sported as wearable fashion items.

In Sawad Brooks' work, the relationship between physical movement and representation is explored through the less obviously physical interfaces of the mouse and screen. But by incorporating unfamiliar navigation techniques, the user is reminded that there is always a physical connection between themselves and the interface. Without attempting to replicate real-world activity, Brooks uses a vocabulary of repetitive mouse movements that have little in common with usual navigation. These movements are an exaggeration of the learning process that the user goes through with any new software, learning how to time the clicks, drags and shifts to move their representations around the screen. But in Brook's work mouse movements are forced to be erratic, and are more tangentially connected with the legibility of the work itself than the traditional point-and-click.

In Focus, one of the Java interfaces in Lapses and Erasures, the user has to frantically drag the mouse backwards and forwards to enlarge a window that reveals text underneath. No matter how hard or fast the mouse moves, the window only opens up enough to reveal a section of the text, often from different lines. This makes

reading a physical act, an act of navigation, rather than narration. The eye cannot follow the expected left-right path and so has to skip over the surface of the text as if it were a physical object, a map revealed through hand-eye co-ordination.

Successful interfaces by necessity have to become invisible, but this does not occur without the user adopting new physical and mental patterns. There is a network of technological, social and physical relationships between the author and the user that an interface has to negotiate in order for it to be adopted widely. The flat icons of the computer desktop have proved to be much more effective than textual or even three-dimensional alternatives. This proves that the representation of data-space does not necessarily have to reflect real

as a hyphen to suggest that a union has occurred between two closely knit communities. 'Brad' has all but lost its 'ford' to Burnley, and Leeds has moved up

experiences. Users adopt, adapt and incorporate interfaces
until they become subliminal, whether it is typing on a
keyboard or driving a car. Sustained participation is the
process that makes the interface invisible, but can also
make 'natural' a series of assumed preferences that should
be regularly interrogated. Adapting, perverting and
generally abusing the purpose of the interface opens up
these choices again, and re-introduces the character of the
individual user – highlighting the grain of the voice in what
must always, by the conditions of use, be a two-way
conversation.

REFERENCES:

(1)   Steven Johnson, Interface Culture, Harper Collins 1997
(2)   from Presence and participation in network art, essay
posted to the nettime mailing list, June 1998
(3)   from an interview between IOD and Geert Lovink posted
to the nettime mailing list, April 1998
(4)   'net.art' is a term that started to be used in 1997 to
describe the activities of network-native artists like Heath
Bunting, Vuk Cosic, Jodi and IOD. It first gained currency
amongst contributors to international digital culture
mailing lists like nettime, 7-11 and rhizome, and despite
consistent attempts to ridicule or replace the term, it
persists as the most common genre title.
(5)   From an interview with IOD's Matthew Fuller, posted to
the nettime mailing list, February 1999.

Matt Locke

far too close to York. Maybe they will reform as a Greater City, re-mark themselves

on to the map in a heavier, bolder, more indelibly printed black — a blacker black

PREVIOUS SPREAD / ABOVE

Steve Hawley & Jonathan Allen:
Stone Troupers
Devonshire Street, Sheffield
14 March — 26 April
Video projection
Commissioners: Lovebytes
(Hypertribes)

Four neo-classical heads
overlooking the City centre come
alive with the faces of shoppers,
ravers, homeless people, old and
young; a cross section of the local
community. A video point was set
up in The Forum Café Bar,
opposite the exhibition site, prior
to the exhibition in order to
record the faces of local people.
Video was projected from the
windows and bounced from
mirrors onto the stone faces.

which nothing will shift. Except in time, perhaps, a whiter white. ¶ A whiter white.

A modern-day obsession with cleanliness. ¶ N.B. I might include a section here on

'Ultra', the language of 'Ultra-ism', a play between language where superlatives are stacked together to extend the range of possible ideal reference. As a whiter white increases the already absurd notion of whiteness as a whiter white. A new improved formula complete with an after-glow which would bring me back to the washing line, bouncing sheets and flapping bath towels and a Richard of York creating whiteness as an aura. And whiteness is an artistic pretension made flesh (as if that were possible), by Malevitch in His White on White canvas or Ben

Granular Synthesis: Pol
Hull Arena and Cream, Liverpool
8 September – 9 October
For the creation of Pol, Granular
Synthesis digitally processed data
recorded with vocalist Diamanda
Galas.
Commissioner: Hull Time Based Arts
(Lucid)

**Presented with a single frame or
within the single frame in a long
sequence of audio and video, the
audience are subjected to a heavy
onslaught of stimuli, bombarded
with light, video and audio
projection.**

Nicholson in those reliefs.¶ The town and city centres of the old industrial North
are no longer dirty. They are clean. Tarted up, pedestrianised, far too consumer

friendly, they only play at being dirty. All of that Victorianesque municipal
brutality has been salvaged and converted to look really nice. The old wrought

Grennan and Sperandio:
Buried Treasures
Grantham, Durham, York and
Berwick Train Stations
Available from October onwards
Comic Book
Commissioning organisation:
Impressions Gallery (On-Line)

**A comic book describing out-of-
the-way stories about four towns
on the London-Edinburgh railway
line, as told by members of the
public.**

iron pavilions have become homogenised shopping lane rows of Thorntons, Penhaligans, Mulberrys, Ravels, Blazers, Body Shops, Jigsaws and Nexts all next to an occasional Harry Ramsden's original Fish and Chip shop or a Wendy Burger.¶ And what about a decent cup of coffee? It is too easy, even on the Station platform. A Cafe Select offers a warm and friendly service. Would I like any nutmeg or cinnamon?¶ *'Any what?'*¶ *'Any nutmeg or cinnamon on top?'*¶ And a pastry, croissant or pain chocolat. No! What if I really fancied a massive mug of tea with

a cheese and ham barm-cake dolloped in piccalilli. This isn't like being at home. It's like abroad. As I remember, there were only two spices Up North. Salt and Pepper.¶ The culture has changed. Inevitably it must. The word culture, from a Latin word 'cultura', means 'to till the soil'.¶ The map which I want to use is out of date. It always has been. My Grandfather's map was printed in 1933 and I was born in 1960. There are no motor ways marked on the map, only A and B roads. A lot has changed in Britain since that time to alter the accuracy of the map. A

Jane Brettle: Fallen

Henry Moore Institute, Leeds

2 — 10 November

Digital photography, 35 mm film

projection

Commissioners: Photo 98

A translucent image of a wing in endless and silent motion moved across the facade of the building, animating the gallery's exterior and the night-time city. The architectural context for the installation was provided by the adjacent war memorial and the polished black granite surface of the Institute, which acted as the `screen` for the projection during its duration.

massive expansion of the size of the population and great demographic shifts have reorganised the patterns of most peoples lives. And Britain is no longer the possessive mother that She once was when over a third of the World Map was coloured in the same 'pretty' pink.¶ My Grandfather's map is crumbling away in

Stephen Willats: Creativeforce
Mappin Art Gallery, Sheffield,
Hillsborough and Manor libraries
11th July, for 3 years
3 interactive installations,
photography, text, specially
designed infomation and
communication computer
programmes
Commissioner: Mappin Gallery

Photographic diaries of local
people's journeys across the city
become pictorial pieces of a
game to be assembled by people
accessing three computer
terminals located across
Sheffield. Presented as an
interactive installations where
the sub-text is one of co-
operation and compromise, each
participant (stationed at each
terminal in the three different
sites) needs the agreement of the
other two participants before
being able to proceed to the next
question. The questions asked of
each player require them to
select a corresponding image or
statement which they feel most
accurately fits the question.

my hands.¶ He first came over to Britain as a boy in 1913 with his father from their home, a small farm off the West-Coast of Ireland. They and boat loads of other Paddies came across to Britain each year to form a part of a migratory pattern of seasonal re-deployment of the Irish work-force. A pattern that had been established for centuries by British land-owners who saw Ireland as a place to build romantic castles for summer retreats, and as a breeding ground for race horses, hounds, scullery maids, nurses, prize fighters and navvies.¶ He and the

Peter McCaughey: X
(Cardiovascular System)
Odeon cinema, York
Throughout June
35 mm film
Commissioning organisation:
Impressions Gallery (Organic City)

**A three minute long 35mm film
trailer shown alongside other
trailers in Odeon cinema. In
perfect imitation of the genre, the
`trailer` hints at a greater mystery:
the subject of the first X-ray
movie of a pumping heart, the
subject later to die of radiation
poisoning.**

other men dug their way through enormous tracts of land which other men filled
with a continuous network of roads, canals, railway lines and sewerage systems
that would extend Britain's cities into towns and so on and on. When the winter set
in they returned to their homes, families and farms with hopefully enough cash to
make it through the following seasons. Thus they maintained a way of life that to
many on the outside, may have seemed mean, harsh, even backward.¶ Travelling
by steam train through Lancashire and Yorkshire must have been a shocking

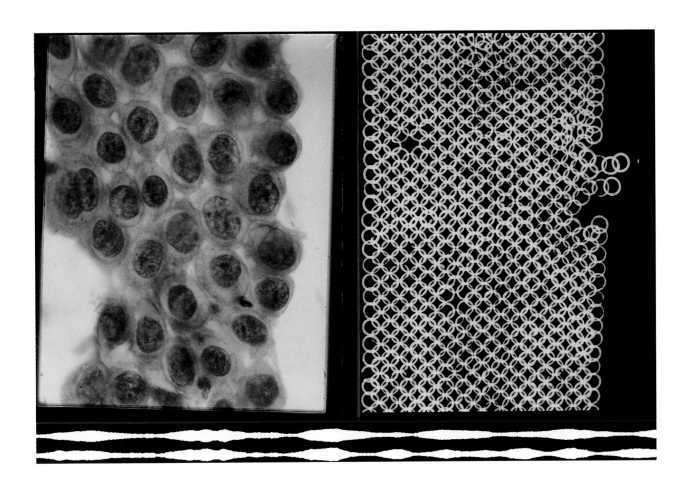

experience for my Grandfather. The smoke of industrial progress obscuring the

view out of the window of half covered municipal domes, church spires mounting

parish clock after parish clock with no end in sight to the serried ranks of brick

filled lanes curving around the blackened hill-sides as homes going on and on

Premium Leisure
(aka Non Axiomatic Living):
Remote Systems
Ponds Forge International
Sports Centre
14 March — 26 April
Sound installation
Commissioners: Lovebytes
(Hypertribes)

An interactive sound installation located at Pond's Forge Sports Centre. Visitors to the exhibition were able to trigger sounds adding to an electronic sound composition, audio 'snap shots' of their movement creating a montage of sound and movements for each day.

forever and ever, and away into a distance that to him was still unknown. My

Grandfather's home had until this time provided a view over three thatched cottages facing out toward the vastness of the Atlantic Ocean.¶ My Grandfather gave me a map which he worked hard all of his life to make obsolete. He was not an artful man. I don't imagine that he gave me the map to preserve as a treasure, nor to re-form it as a reminder of himself. I think that he gave me the map to use but only for as long as it would remain useful.¶ For me to ever attempt to capture his past, is perhaps as futile as me ever attempting to re-capture this, my own

Neil Swanson and
Susan Trangmar:
Take Heart Roof Garden
Jubilee Building, F Floor, Leeds
General Infirmary
Permanent
Fibre-optic lighting, garden
planting, wood, steel
Commissioner: Pavilion and The
United Leeds Teaching Hospital
(Heart and Mind)

Leeds' first roof garden draws on
both the aesthetic and
horticultural inspiration of a
coastal landscape through its
plants and materials.

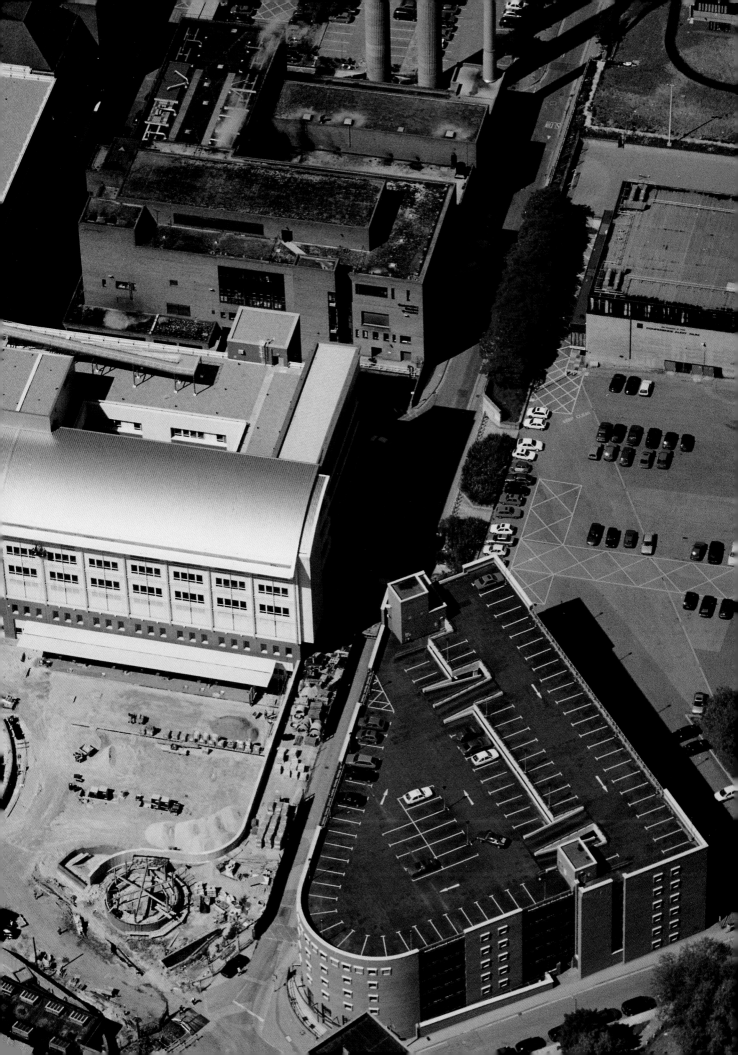

Janet Hodgson:

Every Picture Tells A Story

Situated in the Gilbert Scott Link
corridor, Leeds General Infirmary
Permanent lightboxes
Commissioner: Pavilion and The
United Leeds Teaching Hospital
(Heart and Mind)

**The work consists of 23 trompe-
l'oeil light boxes of surreal images
derived from stories of hospital
life told by hospital staff, placed
appropriately in the architectural
details of the corridor; chickens,
canaries, an old fire bucket.
Although the originator of each
story is listed, the stories
themselves are confidential.**

present.¶ In 1913, just as my grandfather was setting out to travel away from his

home a young painter called Marcel Duchamp went into a shop in Paris and

Pierre D'Avoine and

Catherine Elwes: Car Park Greeting

Multi-storey car park, Calverly Street,

Leeds General Infirmary

Permanent

Banner

Commissioner: Pavilion and The

United Leeds Teaching Hospital

(Heart and Mind)

A monumental secular image of a

mother and child, their hands

raised in a gesture of greeting.

purchased a bicycle wheel. He didn't buy the wheel to attach to a bicycle. Instead

he took it to his studio and attached it to a stool. For two years Duchamp sketched

the shadows of this wheel as it spun around in motion creating a series of

projected shadows on to the side of the walls of his studio.¶ What sense he might have gathered from this process, a kind of naive cinema, is recorded as evidence in the selection of notes and drawings which have subsequently been produced as thousands if not hundreds of thousands of pages of re-production.¶ The Work was not titled until 1915, after Duchamp had left Paris to re-settle himself in New York. Here, it must have suddenly occurred to him that he had already made a significant gesture, significant in some sense as it might relate to art, to the process and re-production of the work as Art. By fastening the wheel to the stool,

Tessa Elliott: Corpuscle 2
(Epitheliium System - Skin)
7 - 8 April 1999
Hospitium, Museum Gardens, York
Neural network, radio buoys
Commissioning organisation:
Impressions Gallery (Organic City)

Donated images of footprints are shown on plasma screens and manipulated by a neural network which draws its data from cameras which monitor the speed, direction and colour of traffic through the four bars in the city walls.

Duchamp had rendered both items obsolete as they could no longer function in any practical manner other than in the sense of demonstrating his own artistic notion.¶ Duchamp renamed the bicycle wheel and stool as an aside from their ordinary common noun status. The bicycle wheel and the stool became the 'Bicycle Wheel' a proper noun and a single work of art. And all that remained for him was

Tessa Elliott: Corpuscle 1
(Epitheliium System - Skin)
27 November
Lendal Bridge, York
Computer generated projection,
small boats
Commissioning organisation:
Impressions Gallery (Organic City)

Images of the soles of feet are
projected onto the River Ouse.
Detectors located in little boats
under a bridge over the river
monitor the flow of the water,
and this data is utilised to direct
the animation of the feet
downstream.

to prove this notion to a wider audience. So he returned to Paris in order to retrieve the object and allow the form to meet and match the title.¶ But on his return he found out that the object had vanished as his sister-in-law had thrown it away as just some more of 'Marcel's useless old clutter'. Duchamp re-made the piece as best he could by repeating the original gesture. And the rest of course is history.

**Rebecca Cummins: Hull Obscured
and Liquid Scrutiny**

30 August – 27 September
The Warren Centre, Hull
Sewerby Hall, Bridlington
Pin-hole cameras, workshops
Commisioner: Hull Time Based Arts
(Lucid)

**Pin-hole cameras were made
from found materials such as a
telephone booth and a wheely
bin. In Liquid Scrutiny eleven
periscope/camera obscuras were
presented based on a 17th century
camera obscura in the shape of a
goblet – an ingenious device for
observing others closely without
their knowledge.**

A history of Modern and Conceptual art, which to some extent began at the moment when he first fastened a spinning wheel to a stool and began to trace the projected shadows.¶ My Grandfather eventually re-settled in Manchester, on the flick and toss of a coin, a heads to Britain or a tails to America.¶ I can remember him

Peter Richards: Pinhole Cameraman
Sewerby Hall, Hull
August 25th - 31st
Pin-hole camera
Commissioner: Hull Time Based Arts
(Lucid)

A marquee erected to function as a pinhole camera sited in the grounds of the estate becoming part of the summertime public activities; weddings, cricket matches and a car rally. Art historical paintings were the subject matter of the images.

spending the last ten years of his life sitting quietly, and to some extent contentedly, by the synthetically luxurious warmth of a three bar electric coal

LUX
AND
ENLIGHTENMENT

effect fire. The light coming through and between the worn chenille curtains that were always three quarters of the way drawn provided only a modest addition to

In the latter half of the twentieth century the historical assumption that temporary exhibitions should be located in the gallery and that permanent public installations are the province of monuments has been questioned. Increasing attempts have been made to shift the site of temporary exhibitions from the inside of galleries and museums to the outside streets that housed those buildings. This 'beyond the gallery' became, in some sectors, a kind of mantra. With key words like 'accessibility' and 'reaching new audiences', Photo 98 certainly tapped into this emergent value of public art. Locating work beyond the gallery space raises interesting questions about the relationship of photography to the visual arts in general, to the public and about the function of photography within and across public spaces.

One stock response to such projects is that it is all very well that art can be removed from the gallery, from the institutional building itself, but, it is argued, this does not necessarily remove art from the discourse of art. To do this, to remove a work of art from art, the artwork would have to be understood as belonging to another category, seen as something else like, for example, those images which would tend to surround any intervention on the street, put to work in the service of advertising or information. In other words art seen as an advert, or like an advert. So when art is put in a public place it thus risks, or creates, an interesting tension by performing a function as a kind of statement which potentially falls in, outside or between expected categories of discourse. Thus one argument for public art is that when placed outside the buildings of art, art has the possibility of interrupting other discourses. But this is also to put the work at a risk of being subsumed by one or more different discourses and in the end no one know who is speaking to who about what. In any sense, none of these issues or ideas make the work automatically more accessible for a wider audience. Nor does public art guarantee a greater understanding of anything.

However, the sense of an institutional cul-de-sac within the art gallery felt by those who wish to escape it is the representation of what elsewhere would be seen as a drive for freedom against limitation. This 'unable to see beyond' what can be done within the gallery indicates that there is perhaps at least a perception of a 'crisis' in the institution of the art gallery. Whether right or wrong, it is such implicit sentiments which partially kindle interest in and precipitate the activities of public art. It is appropriate here then to ask what kind of use is made of art or image-work presented 'beyond the gallery'. What function does it serve? In what way might what art happens outside the gallery illuminate what is or is not going on inside the gallery?

Paul Bradley's twenty metre image of a burning candle projected on the Dean Clough Arts Centre in Halifax, burnt its way slowly through the year of 1998. The candle is a basic technological device for producing a sustained and regular light and as such is representative of the primary requirement for silver based photography — a light source.

the flickering orange glow of the fires un-dying ember. Above the hearth, a framed photographic print of a small white-washed thatched cottage, poised on the edge

Christina McBride's luminescent tape 'light drawing' on a 1760s Orangery in Wakefield is produced by light being received and stored by the luminescent tape which then emanates the architectural features and outline of the building as a light drawing. Whereas the candle is an image which projects light, the tape is dependent on an absorption of light once light has been received - ultra-violetly. Lux, lumen, and light. Both installations employ an idea of enlightenment. Light and enlightenment, without pushing this too literally, are connected in the history of Western thought as a 'way out' of where we are now. Vision and light are privileged registers of knowledge. To see is to move out of ignorance and into the light. In the city dark spaces are supposedly rendered safe by illuminating them. But here in these two installations light has a different relation to knowledge. By returning the issue of photography to its essence — as a question of light — the work (and we) can begin to think about what the relation is between light, knowledge and enlightenment.

At one level both pieces of work can be said to make interventions into the existing public spaces. They draw attention to the buildings in ways that had simply not been seen before. This is a local and specific, limited and spectacular event. Ephemeral and particular, this new

experience of these places given by the works can also be read as emblematic of something else that is going on. After all why on earth would someone want to project a large picture of a candle burning on a building or stick tape all over another one? What kind of reason is at stake in this art? It is not self-evident or 'obvious'.

The candle turns Dean Clough into a steady stream of light, as a constant source of illumination, that is, until the candle burnt out at the end of the year of Photo 98. Analogies with an Olympian torch could be forgiven. The luminescent tape turns the architecture into a baroque parody of itself. This illumination is further ironized by the title given to the piece as 'Urban Facades: Cultivation' — when seen in relation to the present purpose of the building as headquarters for the agency of public arts. Cultivation, a word which speaks of agricultural labour and cultural knowledge, and the title of the candle piece, Tomorrow, forever and never can both be seen as a dry comment on Photo 98 itself. Or more productively, they can be seen at another level as a symptom of a perceived crisis in the art gallery. And at yet another level both projects face the unspoken promise or threat of new technology. As an image, the candle, whatever the form of its projection remains an image from the past and of the past. Candles are for leisure and are far from the new electronic industries of imaging technologies. It is not that candles are antiquated, they are just not so central anymore, in fact ever since electricity was piped into our homes. The glow of the luminescent tape is like that of the twentieth century neon, albeit sharper and quintesentially modern. Yet however these are read, both of them, as light picture and as light drawing, create a visual deception. They produce an image where there was none. This is symptomatic of what, I have argued elsewhere, of something we are experiencing as a kind of Baroque Space. In the Baroque age, celestial frescos, anamorphic distortions, the painted

of an emerald green hillside and set against a pale turquoise sky that gradually dissolved through a milky glaze of what appeared to be a low lying mist, into a

illusions of doors on walls where there was really only a wall, all contributed to the sense of a play with what was once a logic of (Renaissance) similitude. Today, Baroque Space is a cultural space in which the status of images is changing, becoming less certain, where photography no longer guarantees the re-production of existing things and can dis or re-orientate objects and things. This disturbance is caused by the new capacities for illusion of the computer. The desire to escape the gallery in these installations is nevertheless a paradoxical play of light literally on institutions of art, the Art Centre and public arts, which through the process has, perhaps unwittingly, revealed light as chimera. The illuminations stand as evidence of something where in fact there is nothing but light. As a child might reach for the illuminating voice of its parent in a darkened and strange place, the point of light, from which reflections emerge draws the moth. The image of something where there is nothing covers over the hole of existence. The technological inventions that humans have made for themselves and in which they can insert themselves to receive flickering lights, (the cinema, television, the computer) perpetuate an imaginary presence through the image.

David Bate

deeper turquoise sea. If this view of the cottage was any sort of reminder to him, what was it a reminder of, a way of looking forward or a way of looking back, a

Graham Gussin: Billboards

Sandy, Bedfordshire, Grantham,
Lincolnshire and Bentley, Yorkshire
24 October – 20 November
Billboards
Commissioning organisation:
Impressions Gallery (On-Line)

**Three works for billboards sites
depicting imaginary `proposals`;
technical drawings for future
and unspecified sites
provocatively placed on
billboards situated in greenfield
sites adjacent to the railway line.**

view in a new home or a view of an old home.¶ The John Hinde studio postcard of
the Billiard Room in Filey is now propped up against my computer. It is blotted by

Alicia Felberbaum and
Roshini Kempadoo and
Fiona Russell in association with
PEEL (Design): Future Looms
Web site:
http//www.channel.org.uk/futurelooms
Commissioning organisation:
Pavilion and IRIS

A web site of archive footage,
audio-clips and personal
reminiscences that traces the twin
themes of industrial decline and
the promise of technological
renaissance.

a blue-tacky stain which still obscures Skipton and Ilkley but the message remains

clear.¶ Proust writes in Swannsway (the first volume of his novel In Search of Lost

Mark Dion and Morgan Puett:
York Ladies' Field Club
National Railway Museum, York
February - September 1999
Photographs and installation
Commissioning organisation:
Impressions Gallery (On-Line)

A series of photographic tableaux
showing the seven members of
the fictional York Ladies' Field
Club. The portraits are based in
the exact style of the late
Victorian studio portrait, and
each one based on the specialist
interest of the character e.g.
ornithologist, anthropologist.
The photographs have been
modelled by contemporary
curators.

Time): *'I feel that there is much to be said for the Celtic belief that the souls of*
those whom we have lost are held captive in some inferior being, in an animal, in

ORNITHOLOGY
Henrietta Simcoe

DION & PUETT STUDIO   SANCROFT WAY N.R.M. YORK

CONCHOLOGY
Arabella Bell

DION & PUETT STUDIO   SANCROFT WAY N.R.M. YORK

ANTHROPOLOGY
Mrs Herbert Fowler

DION & PUETT STUDIO   SANCROFT WAY N.R.M. YORK

LEPIDOPTERY
Mrs E.W. Fowler

DION & PUETT STUDIO   SANCROFT WAY N.R.M. YORK

PORTER
Sir R. Cornelius Boggs

DION & PUETT STUDIO   SANCROFT WAY N.R.M. YORK

GEOLOGY
Edith Huntington

DION & PUETT STUDIO   SANCROFT WAY N.R.M. YORK

PALEONTOLOGY
Mrs Henry Buckmore

DION & PUETT STUDIO   SANCROFT WAY N.R.M. YORK

BOTANY
Miss Amelia West

DION & PUETT STUDIO   SANCROFT WAY N. R. M. YORK

a plant, in some inanimate object, and so effectively lost to us until the day (which to many never comes) when we happen to pass the tree or obtain the object which forms their prison. Then they call us by our name, and as soon as we have recognised their voice the spell is broken, they have overcome death and return to share our life.' ¶ The message written on a card addressed by my Mother to her parents on the other side of an image chosen by her, of a place that would represent a holiday which I can't remember. But as I look at the card a memory

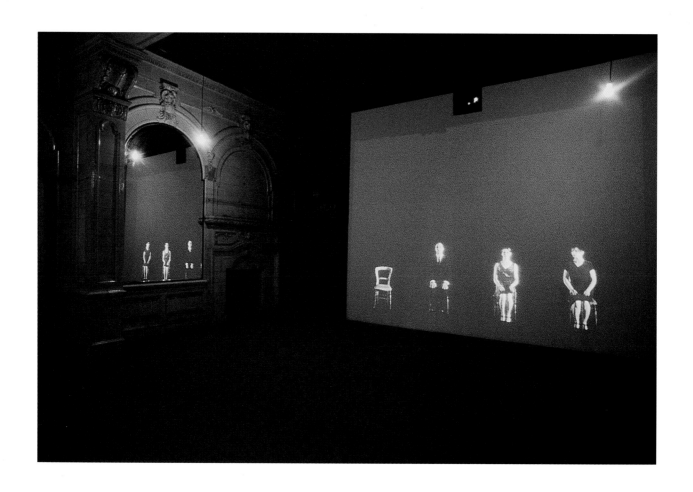

Simon Biggs: The Waiting Room
The Old Dining Room, Platform 1,
Sheffield Station
24 October — 20 November
Video and audio Instalation
Commissioner: Site Gallery, Sheffield
(Shunted)

An interactive audio visual
environment consisting of two
digital video projections by Simon
Biggs with sound by Stuart Jones.
One projection consists of what
appears to be a traditional
waiting room. As viewers enter,
interact with and leave the work
so similarly will a number of
virtual people who appear to sit,
fidget, wait, look at the viewers
and then depart.

comes flooding back.¶ In 1955 John Hinde established a postcard manufacturing business which has sold over 50 million original copies of images of Britain and Ireland throughout the World. These views survive as an image of a place where

Mike Lawson Smith:
Vanishing Points of View.
Union Street, Sheffield
14 March — 26 April
Digital video projection
Commissioners: Lovebytes
(Hypertribes)

An outdoor digital video projection.
The piece displays digitised photo
portraits of supporters of both
Sheffield United and Sheffield
Wednesday football teams, in
ascending order by age. As the
portraits slowly track across
frame, a sensor detects audience
movement and activates a window
of video footage showing each
supporter's team in action.

we all might have been or where we all might have thought that we had been.
Hinde made the ordinary into something quite extra-ordinary. He perfected nature
as it might appear to have been captured within the form of his original

photographic composition. Hinde scores through this original composition, touching and re-touching it up, so that the eventual image will represent the original form in at least a thousand other stereotypes. In truth he re-arranged the truth.¶ Hinde created an image of the past, To Share Our Life, for some time in the

Brighid Lowe: Untitled
Poster sites on the Train Station
and throughout Sheffield
24 October — 20 November
Poster
Commissioner: Site Gallery,
Sheffield (Shunted)

**A black and white poster shows a
giant corporate hand, pushing a
miniaturised, money-filled,
crystal train: a train which in
reality was purchased from a £1
shop.**

future. And Our Life is life burdened by a collective sense of the same identity. As
if we could ever be re-collected, restored or referred to by any inanimate object. A
moment caught, captured is a well known but a worn-out cliché.¶ Hinde plays
with a perception of time in relation to place in order to mass-produce a common

Frances Hegarty & Andrew Stones: Seemingly So, Evidently Not, Apparently Then

The Old Waiting Room, Platform 1, Sheffield Station
24 October — 20 November
Video projection
24 October — 20 November

An old, tiled waiting room suffused with rose-coloured light is used as a site in which to present a ghostly 'apparition' by technological means. A single projected video image showed a live CCTV relay of events on Platform 1, although mixed into the image are an old clock, and a woman dressed in a bizarrely exaggerated Victorian costume who repeatedly walks away along the platform.

and 'shared' perspective. Clare Cryan says of Hinde in Hindesight: '*He was very certain, not that he thought his photography was artistically wonderful but that it was exactly what the market needed. To me it was a very Victorian way of thinking about the market, but there is no doubting its success. I say Victorian because it*

seemed to me to be arrogant at the time to be so sure that you knew exactly what
people wanted. But he did and at the time he was right, they did want idealised
pictures with overblown colour.'¶ Hinde had an impeccable sense of timing and
Warhol had an impeccable sense of doubt: '*Whenever I'm interested in something,*
I know the timing's off, because I'm always interested in the right thing at the
wrong time. I should be getting interested after I'm not interested any more.'¶
Warhol constantly drawing upon anachronisms in his work. He caricatured a

Marysia Lewandowska: Must Go
Leeds and London Train Stations
December
Publication
Commissioning organisation:
Impressions Gallery (On-Line)

**A free publication distributed at
W.H.Smith's in London and Leeds
railway stations based on the
experience of shopping
accompanied by handy hints on
ways to save money on consumer
durables.**

modern world in a very old fashioned way. In 1962 he produced a series of
paintings based on paint-by-number kits. These paintings may be seen as an

ironic tribute to an old fashioned and homely pastime, or as an indictment of a
bourgeois and academic art world.¶ 'Do It Yourself (Landscape).'¶ 'Do it Yourself

(Seascape).'¶ 'Do it Yourself (Narcissus).'¶ The images appear as half-hearted,

NED   DENIED

John Kippin:

Histories of the Imagination

The Rotunda and Scarborough Castle,
Scarborough
13 June — 4 October
Objects cast in resin, book,
photographic installation
Commissioners: Photo 98

**A work in three parts; resin blocks
containing contemporary objects
set into the grounds of
Scarborough Castle, a 360 degree
photographic panel showing the
broad sweep of the Castle grounds
and visitors installed in the
interior room of the circular
Rotunda Museum and the book
Histories of the Imagination which
contained essays on the
presentation of history and
fictional stories looking at what we
learn or interpret from preserved
and accidentally discovered
objects. The book appeared in an
edition of 12,000 which was made
freely available to the public at the
Castle and the Rotunda.**

half-started and half-finished. Incomplete in some sense, or in between that

INVENTED   FORGO

sense, as a demonstration of his own ambiguity, his own indefinite sense. Warhol

PRIVATE

is attempting to paint a real fake painting, hand-rendering after a mechanical

Martin Cottis and Charlie Tymms:
Zoetrope
Workshops in Hull
18 — 27 July
Zoetrope
Commissioner: Hull Time Based Arts
(Lucid)

The artists worked over a three
week period to execute a series of
workshops with local schools,
making and presenting a working
8ft high zoetrope, eventually
appearing in the street.

reproduction. He is parodying an already well-known parody, placing himself in a sticky position. Warhol is acting as an artist, or as a do-it-yourself narcissus.¶ What is going on between the coloured shapes and the numerically coded patterns, which comes first, or perhaps both at the same time? There is something of the boys bedroom about these paintings. Warhol's bedroom, back home in Pittsburgh. A return to, or a stagnation in a notion of his own adolescent routines.¶ 'Do it Yourself (Narcissus).'¶ Warhol's father, a coal miner, a construction worker. And

his mother cutting out crepe paper flowers and selling them in recycled cans from door-to-door, while he remained at home, in the bedroom, clipping out his favourite stars and pasting them all back down, together again.¶ As if in 1962 Warhol has decided to let go of all of the clutter in his mind. After the D. I. Y. paintings a series of silk-screen prints of creased, folded and scattered bank notes, followed by stacks of soup cans, torn labels, perforated warning stickers, Handle with Care-Glass-Thank You, postage stamps, savings stamps and a bundle

of cash tied up with string and pushed into a can, presumably for safe keeping.
Shelves, cupboards and drawers full of this endless and obsessive collection.

**The Appropriated Frame
Artists: Franklyn Rodgers;
Joy Gregory; Dave Lewis;
Roshini Kempadoo;
Armet Francis; Yinka Shonibare;
Maxine Walker; Faisal Abdu Allah;
Clement Cooper; Ajamu;
Rotimi Fani-Kayode;
Peter Max Kandhola; Anthony Lam;
Roy Mehta; Sunil Gupta;
Eileen Perrier; Dawoud Bey;
Chila Burman; 21st Century Club
DJ's Derek Richards and Cleveland
Watkins**
Dark Arches, Granary Wharf, Leeds
23 July
Digital video
Commissioners; Autograph

**An event fusing DJ-mixed sound
with visuals, and texts by
Professor Stuart Hall, Derek
Bishton and Mark Sealy looking at
images of black identity and
representation in photography as
it stands now.**

Warhol re-presenting the trimmings of an old fashioned home as a recreation of his
own fantasies.¶ The several diagrams of how a man would dance the Tango, and

**Nigel Maudsley and
Christos Magganas - Sub*****:
(Skeletal System - Bones)**
Coppergate, York
18 - 24 December
3 man-hole covers, computer
generated animation
Commissioning organisation:
Impressions Gallery (Organic City)

**Looped high resolution computer
generated animation appear
beneath ground glass screens in
purpose built mounts, set into
garden beds. The original and
appropriated images are derived
from diverse sources (diagrams,
photographs, medical imaging,
text) and refers to central motifs
of arteries, veins, road maps,
tunnels, ISDN lines,
communication systems).**

then row after row of Elvises, Troys, Warrens, Natalies and Marilyns printed as if
they were the posters taken from his bedroom wall, stuck down, rubbed together

and stamped over each other. The individual images starting to blur, as if they were porno-flicks. Pages turned too rapidly, double pages spread too far apart and

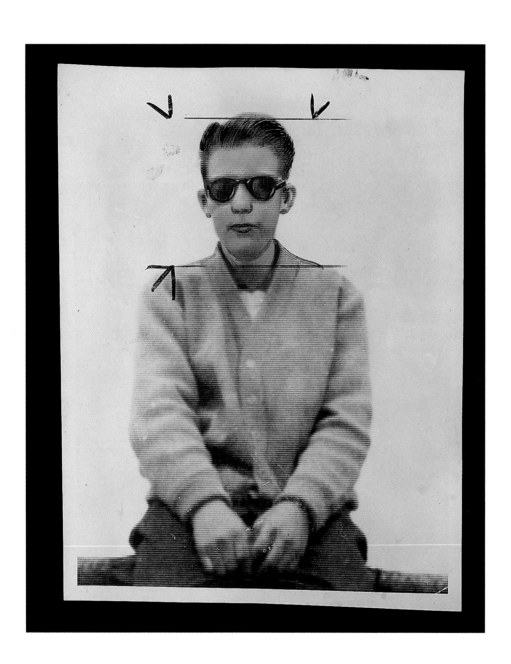

multi-pages multiplied too many times. Images of Elvis, Troy, Warren, Natalie and Marilyn pulled, as repeat patterns or as a tally of several targets. ¶Warhol may

Joachim Schmid:

The Face in the Desert —

Portraits and stories from the

Daily Herald Archive

Architects: Bauman Lyons

Princes Way subway, Bradford

Permanent

Projectors, slides, newspapers

Co-commission National Museum of

Photography, Film and Television

and Photo 98

A project whose theme was the
interplay between photography,
memory and the archive, led
Schmid to select from the huge
photographic archive of the
Daily Herald newspaper housed at
the NMPFT, some of those images
which represent the extraordinary
and bizarre events which
sometimes happen to ordinary
people. These images are
projected on the walls of the
subway and a newspaper is
available from the Museum
bringing the newspaper stories
and images together.
The photographs are typical
family snaps that have been
re-photographed and re-touched
by the newspaper, cropping
away all excess background
and information prior to
publication.

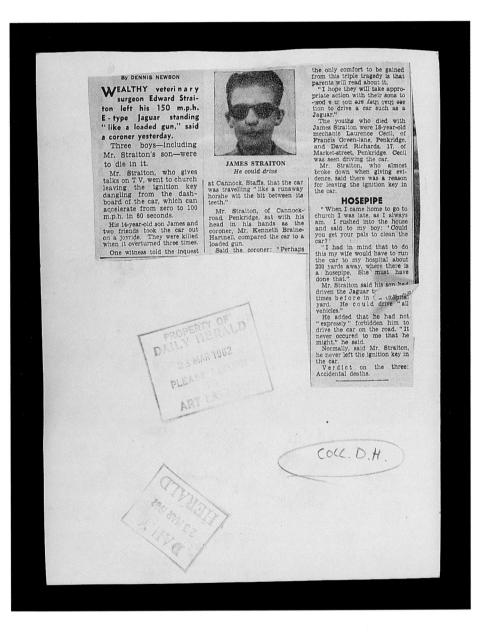

never have heard of John Hinde or ever seen an example of his work, but I think

that he would have recognised his success.¶ *'The people who have the best*

Christina McBride:
Urban facades: Cultivation
The Orangery, Wakefield
8 December – 5 January 1999
photo-luminescent tape, ultra-violet lights
Commissioners: Photo 98

A physical drawing outlining the structure and details of the 18th century Orangery with photo-luminescent tape which glowed brightly when charged by ultra-violet light.

fame are those who have their name on stores. The people with very big stores named after them are the ones I'm really jealous of, like Marshall Field.'¶

Hinde's factory to Warhol's Factory. Hinde's common images to Warhol's images of an elite. Hinde's holiday camp to Warhol's camp. John Hinde retired after he

Melanie Manchot:
Behind the Screen
Tempest Anderson Hall,
Museum Gardens, York
Permanent for 2 years
Silver gelatin prints
Commissioners: Photo 98

The exterior of York's City Screen
cinema provides the setting for a
triptych of silver gelatin images
exploring notions of perception
and the gaze in relation to the
location where they were
displayed — the site of a cinema
backing onto the site of a school
for the blind, now demolished.

had established his name as a leading brand but Warhol continued to un-resolve

himself for a long time after his name had become synonymous with a popular

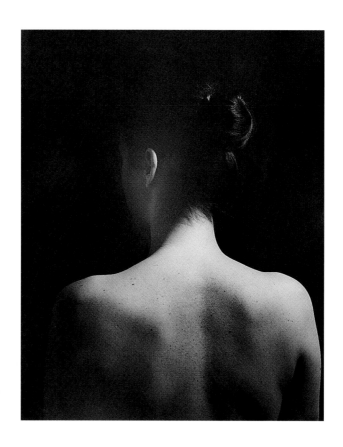

notion of celebrity, fame and fortune.¶   John Hinde was once asked why he
had produced so many postcards of setting suns and he answered: *'Because*

sunsets always sell.'   Bernard Walsh

All quotations used in this work are taken from the following texts: 'In Search of Lost Time', Marcel Proust. Chatto and Windus 1992.
'From A To B And Back Again', Andy Warhol. Picador 1975. 'Hindesight'. The Irish Museum of Modern Art 1993.

LIST OF ARTISTS

Photo 98 Commissions

Felicity Allen
Paul Bradley
Jane Brettle
Jim Buckley
John Kippin
Melanie Manchot
Christina McBride
Helen Sear
Stephen Willats

The Appropriated Frame

Ajamu
Faisal Abdu Allah
Dawoud Bey
Chila Burman
Clement Cooper
Rotimi Fani-Kayode
Armet Francis
Joy Gregory
Sunil Gupta
Roshini Kempadoo
Anthony Lam
Dave Lewis
Peter Max Kandhola
Roy Mehta
Eileen Perrier
Franklyn Rodgers
Yinka Shonibare
Maxine Walker

Hypertribes

Steve Hawley and Jonathan
Allen
Mike Lawson-Smith
Simon Poulter
Premium Leisure
Lulu Quinn
Andrew Stones

Organic City

Bluntcut
Samantha Clark
Tessa Elliott
Nigel Maudsley and
Christos Magganas
Matthew Maxwell

Peter McCaughey
Richard Hylton
Abdul Qualam Aziz
Other Worlds

Future Looms

Alicia Felberbaum
Roshini Kempadoo
Fiona Russell

Heart and Mind

Pierre D'Avoine and
Catherine Elwes
Janet Hodgson
Neil Swanson and
Susan Trangmar

Northern Lights

Joachim Schmid

Lucid

Andy Hazell with
Carolyn Mendelsohn
Mongrel
Granular Synthesis
Heather Ackroyd and
Dan Harvey
Champon Apisuk
Martin Cottis and
Charlie Tymms
Rebecca Cummins
Gina Czarnecki
Lisa Erdman
Peter Richards
Ann Whithurst with
Patric Courtney and
Harry Palmer

Shunted

Simon Biggs
Frances Hegarty and
Andrew Stones
Impossible Theatre
Brighid Lowe
Mark Wallinger

On Line

Mark Dion and
Morgan Puett
Stefan Gec
Grennan & Sperandio
Graham Gussin
Marysia Lewandowska

PUBLIC SIGHTINGS

The artworks shown in this publication were all part of the Public Sightings programme: a total of 60 discrete projects taking place during Photo 98, the UK Year of Photography and the Electronic Image. 1998 was one of the nine `Years of' designated by the Arts Council of England leading up to the Millennium - the Arts 2000 initiative - each dedicated to exploring and raising the profile of a different art-form. The Yorkshire region bid for, and was chosen, to host the Year of Photography and the Electronic Image and an agency, Photo 98, was set up to co-ordinate, commission, fund-raise and market the programme.

Photo 98's key aims included reaching new audiences and raising the profile of creative photography and its role as a medium within contemporary visual arts practice. A key strand within Photo 98 was Public Sightings, a programme of new commissions for sites outside of the gallery context intended to encourage experimentation and question assumptions about where and what a photographic or lens-based artwork could, or should be.

The majority of commissions, although not all, were temporary and many were digitally based; appearing and disappearing across the urban landscapes and web sites of Yorkshire and the UK throughout the Year. While the history of photography has always engendered a continuing debate around issues of identity and representation, Public Sightings was able to extend the arena of engagement by giving space, financial backing and encouragement to artists, particularly those working with new media, to work beyond the virtual, the computer screen and the frame, to engage with the physical realities, demands and vagaries of architectural space, public environments and audience.

Nicola Stephenson
Public Art Manager, Photo 98

PHOTOGRAPHY CREDITS

All Lucid (except Chumpon Apisuk, Rebecca Cummins, and Photosynthesis) — I D 8

Chumpon Apisuk — C. A.

Rebecca Cummins — Philip Rhodes

Photosynthesis — Dan Harvey

All Hypertribes (except Vanishing Points of View) — I D 8

Vanishing Points of View — Mike Lawson-Smith

Jim Buckley: Fold — Tim Smith

All Shunted — Stuart Blackwood

Christina McBride, Urban Facades: Cultivation — Jerry Hardman-Jones

Jane Brettle — Jane Brettle

Felicity Allen: Fallen — Felicity Allen

Paul Bradley: Tomorrow, forever and never — Susan Crowe

John Kippin: Histories of the Imagination — John Kippin

Melanie Manchot: Behind the Screen — Melanie Manchot

Photograph of Louise Brooks in Pandora's Box — G. W. Pabst

Melanie Manchot installation — Tim Smith

Helen Sear: Strata and Labyrinth — Helen Sear

Strata and Labyrinth installation — Helen Sear

Autograph: Appropriated Frame — Jerry Hardman-Jones

All Organic City — Jerry Hardman-Jones

Except for Organic City artists own work where shown: — Peter McCaughey and Matthew Maxwell

Pavilion: All Heart and Mind installations — Martin Peters

Joachim Schmid: The Face in the Desert — Joachim Schmid, National Museum of Photography, Film and TV, Daily Herald Archive

Betty's Tea Rooms, York — Yorkshire Post

Cricket Match — Yorkshire Tourist Board

Yorkshire Landscape — Simon Warner

Power Station — Andrew Cross

Coal mine — British Coal Archive

Stefan Gec — Stefan Gec

Marysia Lewandowska — Marysia Lewandowska

Graham Gussin — Andrew Cross

Rebecca Cummins — Phillip Rhodes

Public Sightings is published by PhotoArts 2000 (Photo 98) for the Year of Photography and the Electronic Image.

This publication
© 1999, PhotoArts2000 (Photo 98)

Images and texts
© 1999, the authors

Editors: Andrew Cross and Simon Grennan
Executive Editor: Nicola Stephenson

Designed by AW @ Axis, Manchester
email: alan@axis.zen.co.uk

ISBN: 0 9535711 0 6

photo 98
Canon

Yorkshire & Humberside
ARTS

Canon is an award winner under the Arts & Business Pairings Scheme for its support of Photo 98. The Pairing Scheme is funded by the Arts Council of England and the Department of Culture, Media and Sport.